P9-DEZ-325

To

From

Date

The quoted ideas expressed in this book (but not Scripture verses) are not, in all cases, exact quotations, as some have been edited for clarity and brevity. In all cases, the author has attempted to maintain the speaker's original intent. In some cases, quoted material for this book was obtained from secondary sources, primarily print media. While every effort was made to ensure the accuracy of these sources, the accuracy cannot be guaranteed. For additions, deletions, corrections, or clarifications in future editions of this text, please write Freeman-Smith, LLC.

Scripture quotations are taken from:

The Holy Bible, King James Version

Holy Bible, New Living Translation, (NLT) Copyright © 1996. Used by permission of Tyndale House Publishers, Inc., Wheaton, Illinois 60189. All rights reserved.

The Message (MSG)- This edition issued by contractual arrangement with NavPress, a division of The Navigators, U.S.A. Originally published by NavPress in English as THE MESSAGE: The Bible in Contemporary Language copyright 2002-2003 by Eugene Peterson. All rights reserved.

International Children's Bible®, New Century Version®. (ICB) Copyright © 1986, 1988, 1999 by Tommy Nelson™, a division of Thomas Nelson, Inc. All rights reserved. Used by permission.

New Century Version®. (NCV) Copyright © 1987, 1988, 1991 by Word Publishing, a division of Thomas Nelson, Inc. All rights reserved. Used by permission.

The Holman Christian Standard Bible™ (Holman CSB) Copyright © 1999, 2000, 2001 by Holman Bible Publishers. Used by permission.

Cover Design & Page Layout by Bart Dawson

ISBN 978-1-58334-495-8

Printed in the United States of America

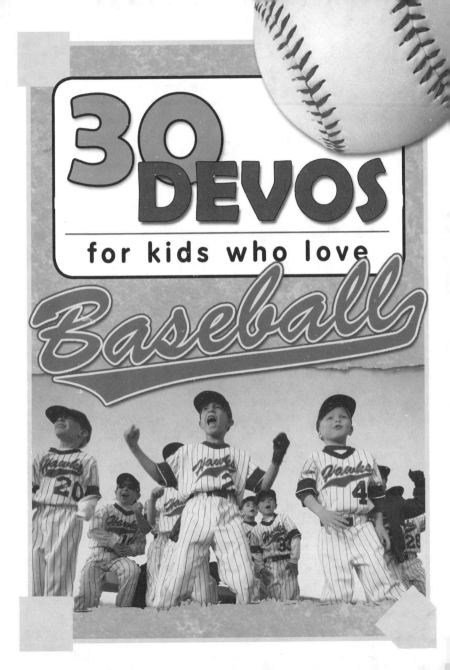

30 DEVOS

for kids who love

Baseball

TABLE OF CONTENTS

Introduction

If your child's bookshelf is already spilling over with a happy assortment of good books for kids, congratulations—that means you're a thoughtful parent who understands the importance of reading to your child.

If your youngster plays baseball, softball, or T-ball, this little book is an important addition to his or her library. It is intended to be read by Christian parents to their young children. The text contains 30 brief devotionals, one for each day of the month. Each chapter consists of a Bible verse, a brief story, kid-friendly quotations (from notable Christian thinkers and baseball legends), fun facts about baseball history, tips for kids, and a prayer. Every devotional reading teaches a little about baseball and a lot about life.

For the next 30 days, take the time to read one chapter each night to your child, and then spend a few moments talking about the chapter's meaning. By the end of the month, you will have had 30 different opportunities to share God's wisdom with your son or daughter, and that's good . . . very good.

If you have been touched by God's love and His grace, then you know the joy that He has brought into your own life. Now it's your turn to share His message with the boy or girl whom He has entrusted to your care. Happy reading! And may God richly bless you and your family now and forever.

CHAPTER 1

If You're a Christian, Play Like One

*Just as you want others to do for you,
do the same for them.*

Luke 6:31 Holman CSB

TODAY'S BIG IDEA!

Since you're a Christian, you should behave like one all the time (including when you're playing baseball).

What does the Bible say about being a good sport? Plenty! God's Word teaches us that we should treat other people like we'd want to be treated if we were in their shoes. And that means that we should be courteous and kind, on the field or off.

Where does kindness start? It starts in our hearts and works its way out from there. Jesus taught us that a pure heart is a wonderful blessing. It's up to each of us to fill our hearts with love for God, love for Jesus, and love for all people. When we do, we are blessed.

Do you want to be the best person you can be? Then invite the love of Christ into your heart and share His love with your family, with your friends, with your teammates, and with your opponents. And remember that lasting love always comes from a pure heart . . . like yours!

When you extend hospitality to others, you're not trying to impress people, you're trying to reflect God to them.

—

Max Lucado

The mark of a Christian is that he will walk the second mile and turn the other cheek. A wise person gives the extra effort, all for the glory of the Lord Jesus Christ.

—

John Maxwell

Be so preoccupied with good will
that you haven't room for ill will.

—

E. Stanley Jones

If we have the true love of God
in our hearts, we will show it
in our lives. We will not have to go
up and down the earth proclaiming it.
We will show it in everything
we say or do.

—

D. L. Moody

NOW HEAR THIS!

You gotta lose 'em some time.
When you do, lose 'em right.

—

Casey Stengel

DID YOU KNOW?

Although Abner Doubleday has often been given credit for "inventing" the game of baseball, historians now agree that there was no single individual who created the game. Baseball probably evolved from the English game of "rounders," an inner-city game that resembled modern-day stickball.

ONE MORE THING TO REMEMBER

Showing good sportsmanship is more important than winning ballgames. God doesn't care whether you win or lose, but He does care how you treat other people. So behave yourself accordingly.

TODAY'S PRAYER

Dear Lord, give me the wisdom
to be a good sport, on the field
and off. Let me be humble when
I win and courteous when I lose,
today and every day.
Amen

CHAPTER 2

Play with the Right Attitude

Set your minds on what is above, not on what is on the earth.

Colossians 3:2 Holman CSB

TODAY'S BIG IDEA!

On the baseball diamond or off, your attitude is important. So guard your thoughts carefully . . . and try not to lose control.

What does the word "attitude" mean? "Attitude" means "the way that you think." And your attitude is important in the game of baseball and in the game of life. Your attitude can make you happy or sad, grumpy or glad, joyful or mad. Your attitude doesn't just control the way that you think; it also controls how you play the game. If you have a good attitude, you'll be a better player. But if you have a bad attitude, you're more likely to misbehave.

Have you spent any time thinking about the way that you think? Hopefully so! After all, a good attitude is better than a bad one . . . lots better.

You have more control over your attitude than you think. One way you can improve your attitude is by learning about Jesus and about His attitude toward life. When you do, you'll learn that it's always better to think good thoughts, and it's always better to do good things. Always!

Developing a positive attitude means working continually to find what is uplifting and encouraging.

—

Barbara Johnson

A positive attitude will have positive results because attitudes are contagious.

—

Zig Ziglar

All things being equal, attitude wins.
All things not being equal,
attitude sometimes still wins.

—

John Maxwell

Attitude is the mind's paintbrush;
it can color any situation.

—

Barbara Johnson

NOW HEAR THIS!

Take a swing at life now.

—

Mickey Mantle

Associate with those who help you believe in yourself.

—

Brooks Robinson

DID YOU KNOW?

The first significant American baseball team was the New York Knickerbockers. The team formed in 1845 and was composed of doctors, lawyers, and businessmen.

ONE MORE THING TO REMEMBER

A positive attitude leads to positive results;
a bad attitude leads elsewhere.

TODAY'S PRAYER

Dear Lord, I pray for an attitude that
pleases You. Even when I'm angry,
unhappy, tired, or upset, I pray that
I can remember what it means
to be a good person
and a good Christian.
Amen

CHAPTER 3

Be a Good Example

You are young, but do not let anyone treat you as if you were not important. Be an example to show the believers how they should live. Show them with your words, with the way you live, with your love, with your faith, and with your pure life.

1 Timothy 4:12 ICB

TODAY'S BIG IDEA!

Whether you're on the baseball diamond or off it, your friends are watching. So be the kind of example that God wants you to be— be a good example.

When you're playing baseball—or doing anything else—what kind of example are you? Are you the kind of person who shows other kids what it means to be a Christian? Are you a good sport and a team player? And do you always try your hardest? Hopefully so!!!

When you do the right thing, you're bound to be a good example to other kids. And that's good because God needs people like you who are willing to stand up and be counted for Him.

More depends on my walk
than my talk.

—

D. L. Moody

The best evidence of our having
the truth is our walking
in the truth.

—

Matthew Henry

I don't care what a person says
he believes with his lips.
I want to know what he says
with his life and his actions.

—

Sam Jones

Never support an experience
which does not have God as its
source and faith in God
as its result.

—

Oswald Chambers

NOW HEAR THIS!

Success is being truly happy at what you do.

—

Tommy Lasorda

Little League is great because it keeps the parents off the streets.

—

Yogi Berra

DID YOU KNOW?

Professional baseball has been around for a long time. In fact, the first professional baseball teams in America formed in 1868 in a league called the National Association of Base Ball Players.

ONE MORE THING TO REMEMBER

God wants you to be a good example to your family, to your friends, and to the world.

TODAY'S PRAYER

Lord, make me a good example
to my family and friends.
Let the things that I say and do show
everybody what it means to be
a good person and a good Christian.
Amen

CHAPTER 4

Learn to Control Yourself

*So prepare your minds for service
and have self-control. All your hope should
be for the gift of grace that will be yours
when Jesus Christ is shown to you.*

1 Peter 1:13 NCV

TODAY'S BIG IDEA!

When you play sports, you should try to learn self-discipline and self-control. The sooner you learn how to control yourself, the better.

Are you learning how to control yourself on the baseball field and off? If the answer to that question is yes, then you deserve a big cheer because God wants all His children (including you) to behave themselves.

Sometimes, it's hard to be a well-behaved person, especially if you and your teammates become wrapped up in the outcome of a game. But if your teammates misbehave, don't imitate them. Instead, listen to your conscience, and do the right thing . . . RIGHT NOW!

If one examines the secret behind
a championship football team,
a magnificent orchestra,
or a successful business,
the principal ingredient is
invariably discipline.

—

James Dobson

Your thoughts are the determining
factor as to whose mold you are
conformed to. Control your thoughts
and you control the direction
of your life.

—

Charles Stanley

True will power and courage
are not only on the battlefield, but
also in those everyday victories.

—

D. L. Moody

NOW HEAR THIS!

Practice, work hard, and give it everything you've got.

—

Dizzy Dean

Every player should have goals to keep his interest up. Goals should be realistic and they should reflect improvement.

Ted Williams

DID YOU KNOW?

The first professional team composed completely of professional players was the Cincinnati Red Stockings. They began playing in 1869.

ONE MORE THING TO REMEMBER

Sometimes, the best way to control yourself is to slow yourself down. Then, you can think about the things you're about to do before you do them.

TODAY'S PRAYER

Dear Lord, the Bible teaches me that it's good to be able to control myself. Today, I will slow myself down and think about things before I do things. Amen

CHAPTER 5

Don't Be Afraid to Swing Away!

Don't be afraid. Only believe.
Mark 5:36 Holman CSB

TODAY'S BIG IDEA!

Don't be too afraid of striking out. Just swing away, give it your best, and expect the best.

His adoring fans called him the "Sultan of Swat." He was Babe Ruth, the baseball player who set records for home runs and strikeouts. Babe's philosophy was simple. He said, "Never let the fear of striking out get in your way." That's smart advice on the diamond or off.

Of course it's never wise to take foolish risks (so buckle up, slow down, and don't do anything silly). But when it comes to the game of life, you should not let the fear of failure keep you from taking your swings.

Today, ask God for the courage to step beyond the boundaries of your self-doubts. Ask Him to guide you to a place where you can realize your full talents—a place where you can rise above the fear of failure. Ask Him to do His part, and promise Him that you will do your part, too. When you do, there's no limit to the things that you and God, working together, can do.

Fear is a self-imposed prison that will keep you from becoming what God intends for you to be.

—

Rick Warren

Only believe, don't fear. Our Master, Jesus, always watches over us, and no matter what the problem, Jesus will surely overcome it.

—

Lottie Moon

Faith is stronger than fear.

—

John Maxwell

Are you fearful? First, bow your head
and pray for God's strength.
Then, raise your head knowing that,
together, you and God can handle
whatever comes your way.

—

Jim Gallery

NOW HEAR THIS!

If you're afraid, you'll never do the job.

—

Bill Mazeroski

If you don't learn to live with failure, it will kill you as a player.

—

Dave Winfield

DID YOU KNOW?

Old-time baseball players must have been tough. They didn't even start using gloves until about 1875. Ouch!

ONE MORE THING TO REMEMBER

If you're too afraid of failure, you may not live up to your potential. Remember that failing isn't nearly as bad as failing to try.

TODAY'S PRAYER

Dear Lord, even when I'm afraid
of failure, give me the courage to try.
Remind me that with You by my side,
I really have nothing to fear. So today,
Father, I will live courageously
as I place my faith in You.
Amen

CHAPTER 6

Have Fun and Play Happy!

A cheerful heart fills the day with a song.
Proverbs 15:15 MSG

TODAY'S BIG IDEA!

Games are meant to be fun! So while you're playing baseball, don't forget to enjoy yourself.

The game of baseball is meant to be fun—that's why they call it a game. But sometimes, we take our games a little too seriously. We allow ourselves to become so wrapped up in winning and losing that we forget to have fun. And that's a big mistake!

While you're playing baseball—or doing just about anything else, for that matter—have fun. After all, this is the day the Lord has made, and He wants us to celebrate . . . TODAY!

No one is truly happy if he has what he wants, but only if he wants something he should have.

—

St. Augustine

Happiness, like its opposite, is habit-forming.

—

Criswell Freeman

It is not how much we have,
but how much we enjoy,
that makes our happiness.

—

C. H. Spurgeon

God made round faces;
people make 'em long.

—

Anonymous

NOW HEAR THIS!

Generate happiness within yourself.

—

Ernie Banks

There's sunshine, fresh air, and the fans are behind us. Let's play two.

—

Ernie Banks

DID YOU KNOW?

Pitchers weren't allowed to throw overhand until 1884. But the old-timers still threw fast, and a pitcher named Candy Cummings, who played for the Brooklyn Excelsiors, even developed an underhand curveball!

ONE MORE THING TO REMEMBER

The best day to be happy is this one. Don't spend your whole life in the waiting room. Make up your mind to celebrate today.

TODAY'S PRAYER

Dear Lord, You have given me
a priceless gift: the gift of life.
Today I will treasure that gift
and enjoy it.
Amen

CHAPTER 7

Respect Everybody (Including the Other Team!)

*Show respect for all people.
Love the brothers and sisters
of God's family.*

1 Peter 2:17 ICB

TODAY'S BIG IDEA!

You should treat all players with respect. That means you should be kind to your teammates and to the players on the other team.

Do you try to have a respectful attitude toward your teammates? And do you show respect for the players on the other team, too? Hopefully, you can answer these questions with a great, big YES!

The Bible teaches us to treat all people with respect. And showing respect for others is habit-forming: the more you do it, the easier it becomes. So start practicing right now. Say lots of kind words and do lots of kind things, because when it comes to kindness and respect, practice makes perfect.

God shows unbridled delight
when He sees people acting
in ways that honor Him,
when He sees tender love shared
among His people.

—

Bill Hybels

Courtesy is contagious.

—

Marie T. Freeman

When you received Jesus Christ
as your personal Lord and Savior,
you began a relationship
not only with Him but also with
all other Christians.

—

Billy Graham

The Lord Jesus Christ enables us
all to be family.

—

Dennis Swanberg

NOW HEAR THIS!

You always have to believe
in yourself before others
can believe in you.

—

Tommy Lasorda

DID YOU KNOW?

In the late 1800s, championship games were sometimes played between the winners of rival professional leagues. But the first "modern" World Series wasn't held until 1903 when the Boston Americans defeated the Pittsburgh Pirates in a best-of-nine series (Boston won five games to three).

ONE MORE THING TO REMEMBER

Everybody Is a VIP: VIP means "Very Important Person." To God, everybody is a VIP, and we should treat every person with dignity, patience, and respect.

TODAY'S PRAYER

Dear Lord, I will try to show respect
to everybody, starting with
my family and my friends.
And, I will do my best to share
the love that I feel in my heart
for them . . . and for You!
Amen

CHAPTER 8

No Temper Tantrums

Don't become angry quickly,
because getting angry is foolish.

Ecclesiastes 7:9 NCV

TODAY'S BIG IDEA!

If you lose your cool and throw a temper tantrum, you lose. If you keep your cool and don't throw a tantrum, you win!

Temper tantrums are always silly, whether they happen on the baseball diamond, at home, or anyplace in between. And pouting is silly. So, of course, is whining. When we lose our tempers, we say things that we shouldn't say, and we do things that we shouldn't do. And it's too bad!

The Bible tells us that it is foolish to become angry and that it is wise to remain calm. That's why we should learn to control our tempers before our tempers control us.

If your temper gets the best of you . . . then other people get to see the worst in you.

—

Criswell Freeman

Anger is the noise of the soul;
the unseen irritant of the heart.

—

Max Lucado

Anger breeds remorse in the heart,
discord in the home, and bitterness
in the community.

—

Billy Graham

NOW HEAR THIS!

Look at misfortune the same way you look at success. Don't panic.

—

Walter Alston

DID YOU KNOW?

Cy Young, who broke into professional baseball in 1890, went on to become the winningest pitcher in history with 511 victories—it's an unbreakable record. But most folks don't know that Cy also holds the record for the most losses, too. He lost 316 games!

ONE MORE THING TO REMEMBER

No more tantrums! If you think you're about to pitch a fit or throw a tantrum, slow down, catch your breath, and walk away if you must. It's better to walk away—and keep walking—than it is to blurt out angry words that can't be un-blurted.

TODAY'S PRAYER

Dear Lord, help me to keep away from angry thoughts and angry people. And if I am tempted to have a temper tantrum, help me to calm down before I do.
Amen

CHAPTER 9

Don't Be Too Hard on Yourself

Give all your worries and cares to God,
for he cares about what happens to you.

1 Peter 5:6 NLT

TODAY'S BIG IDEA!

If you make a mistake (in baseball or in life), get over it! The sooner you forgive yourself and move on, the sooner you'll start playing better.

Do you make mistakes on the field . . . and off the field, too? Of course you do . . . everybody does. When you make a mistake, you must try your best to learn from it so that you won't make the very same mistake again. And, if you have hurt someone—or if you have disobeyed God— you must ask for forgiveness.

Remember: mistakes are a part of life, but the biggest mistake you can make is to keep making the same mistake over and over and over again.

Father, take our mistakes
and turn them into opportunities.

—

Max Lucado

God is able to take mistakes,
when they are committed to Him,
and make of them something
for our good and for His glory.

—

Ruth Bell Graham

I hope you don't mind me telling
you all this. One can learn only
by seeing one's mistakes.

—

C. S. Lewis

Goals are worth setting
and worth missing.
We learn from non-successes.

—

Bill Bright

NOW HEAR THIS!

Don't look back.
Something might be gaining on you.

—

Satchel Paige

I don't want to make the
wrong mistake.

—

Yogi Berra

DID YOU KNOW?

After Cy Young, the second winningest pitcher of all time is Walter Johnson (417 wins). Johnson played for the lowly Washington Senators from 1907 until 1927. He had a terrific fastball and was considered by many to be the greatest hurler of his day.

ONE MORE THING TO REMEMBER

When you make a mistake, learn something . . . and forgive someone: yourself. Remember, you don't have to be perfect to be wonderful.

TODAY'S PRAYER

Dear Lord, sometimes I make mistakes. When I do, help me learn something, help me forgive myself, and help me become a smarter person today than I was yesterday.
Amen

CHAPTER 10

Listen to Your Conscience

*They show that in their hearts they know
what is right and wrong.*

Romans 2:15 ICB

TODAY'S BIG IDEA!

Whether you're on the baseball diamond or someplace else, listen to your conscience. If you listen to your conscience, you'll do the right thing.

When you know that you're doing what's right, you'll feel better about yourself. Why? Because you have a little voice in your head called your "conscience." Your conscience is a feeling that tells you whether something is right or wrong—and it's a feeling that makes you feel better about yourself when you know you've done the right thing.

Your conscience is an important tool. Pay attention to it!

The more you listen to your conscience, the easier it is to behave yourself. So here's great advice: first, slow down long enough to figure out the right thing to do—and then do it! When you do, you'll be proud of yourself . . . and other people will be proud of you, too.

Your conscience is your
alarm system.
It's your protection.

—

Charles Stanley

It is neither safe nor prudent
to do anything against
one's conscience.

—

Martin Luther

Guilt is a healthy regret
for telling God one thing
and doing another.

—

Max Lucado

One's conscience can only
be satisfied when
God is satisfied.

—

C. H. Spurgeon

NOW HEAR THIS!

You can observe a lot just by watching.

—

Yogi Berra

Study the game, accept advice, keep fit, and above all, save your money.

—

Babe Ruth

DID YOU KNOW?

Boston's Fenway Park, which remains one of America's favorite ballparks, was opened in 1912. So it's not surprising that today, the beloved Fenway is one of the most historic stadiums in all of sports.

ONE MORE THING TO REMEMBER

If you're not sure it's the right thing to do . . . listen to your conscience and talk to your parents—or to your coach.

TODAY'S PRAYER

Dear Lord, You have given me
a conscience that tells me what
is right and what is wrong.
I will listen to that quiet voice so
I can do the right thing today
and every day.
Amen

CHAPTER 11

Don't Quit Playing Until the Game Is Over

*We say they are happy because
they did not give up.*

James 5:11 NCV

TODAY'S BIG IDEA!

If your team falls behind in the early innings, don't give up! Keep on trying your hardest, and make sure your teammates do the same. After all, in baseball, it's never over until the final out.

Sometimes, if your team falls behind, you may be tempted to give up and stop trying. But please resist that temptation!

Jesus finished what He began, and so should you. Jesus didn't give in, and neither should you. Jesus did what was right, and so should you.

Are you facing something that is hard for you to do? If so, remember this: whatever your problem, God can handle it. Your job is to keep working until He does.

Don't quit. For if you do,
you may miss the answer
to your prayers.

—

Max Lucado

The hardest part of a journey
is neither the start nor the finish,
but the middle mile.

—

Vance Havner

We are all on our way somewhere.
We'll get there if we just keep going.

—

Barbara Johnson

Don't give up.
Moses was once a basket case!

—

Anonymous

NOW HEAR THIS!

**Deal with one pitch at a time
and make every one count.**

—

Nolan Ryan

**Experience is a tough teacher.
It gives the test before
giving the lesson.**

—

Vernon Law

DID YOU KNOW?

Babe Ruth, who became a legendary slugger and the greatest homerun hitter of his era, started out as a pitcher! In fact, Babe was one of the finest hurlers of his age, and his World Series pitching record (for the most consecutive scoreless innings) stood for 43 years.

ONE MORE THING TO REMEMBER

When in doubt, keep playing hard until the final out.

TODAY'S PRAYER

Dear Lord, when I'm tempted to quit, give me the courage to keep going. And when the game is over, give me the wisdom to accept the results, no matter the score.
Amen

CHAPTER 12

Try Your Hardest!

*Whatever you do, do it enthusiastically,
as something done for the Lord
and not for men.*

Colossians 3:23 Holman CSB

TODAY'S BIG IDEA!

Wherever you happen to be—whether you're on the baseball diamond or at school or anywhere in between—try to do your best. When you work hard, and keep working hard, you'll earn big rewards.

Whether you're practicing or playing in a game, you know that you should give your best effort. But sometimes, especially when you get tired, you'll be tempted to slow down or give up altogether. Don't do it! Keep trying, even when you're tired or discouraged, or both.

Face facts: Life's biggest rewards aren't likely to fall into your lap. Your greatest accomplishments will probably require plenty of effort, which is perfectly fine with God. After all, He knows that you're up to it, and He has big plans for you. God will do His part to fulfill those plans, and the rest, of course, is up to you.

We must trust as if it
all depended on God and work
as if it all depended on us.

—

C. H. Spurgeon

Few things fire up a person's
commitment like dedication
to excellence.

—

John Maxwell

You can't climb the ladder of life
with your hands in your pockets.

—

Barbara Johnson

Success or failure can be pretty
well predicted by the degree
to which the heart is fully in it.

—

John Eldredge

NOW HEAR THIS!

You'll never reach second base if you keep one foot on first.

—

Vernon Law

The difference between the possible and the impossible lies in a person's determination.

—

Tommy Lasorda

DID YOU KNOW?

Although Babe Ruth was the greatest player of his era (and arguably the greatest player of all time), he only won one MVP award (in 1923). Amazingly, Ruth was the first player ever to hit 30, 40, 50 and 60 home runs in a single season.

ONE MORE THING TO REMEMBER

Sooner or later, practice has a way of paying off (and it's usually sooner).

TODAY'S PRAYER

Dear Lord, when I'm on the baseball diamond, or anywhere else, let me try my hardest. Let me do my best and leave the rest to You.

Amen

CHAPTER 13

Don't Be a Chronic Complainer!

Be hospitable to one another without complaining.

1 Peter 4:9 Holman CSB

TODAY'S BIG IDEA!

On the baseball diamond, you may be tempted to complain about the umpire's calls. But you should resist that temptation. Instead of worrying about bad calls, think about what you can do next to help your team win the game.

When things don't go your way on the baseball diamond, are you tempted to complain? Or pout? Or whine? If so, it's time to change the way you think and the way you behave.

Some kids think that whining is a good way to get the things they want (but hopefully you're wiser than that). In truth, whining doesn't work for long. So if your parents or your coach ask you to do something, don't complain about it. And if there's something you want, don't whine and complain until you get it.

Remember: whining won't make you happy . . . and it won't make anybody else happy, either.

Just as courage is faith in good,
so discouragement is faith in evil,
and, while courage opens
the door to good, discouragement
opens it to evil.

—

Hannah Whitall Smith

Jesus wept,
but he never complained.

—

C. H. Spurgeon

When you're on the verge of
throwing a pity party thanks to
your despairing thoughts,
go back to the Word of God.

—

Charles Swindoll

Shine—don't whine.

—

Anonymous

NOW HEAR THIS!

Never complain. Most people don't care about your troubles, and the rest are glad you've got them.

—

Tommy Lasorda

DID YOU KNOW?

In 1938, Cincinnati Reds pitcher Johnny Vander Meer threw back-to-back no-hitters. On June 11, he no-hit the Boston Bees. Four days later, he did it again to the Brooklyn Dodgers. Amazing!

ONE MORE THING TO REMEMBER

Constant complaining is a bad habit—make sure it's not your bad habit!

TODAY'S PRAYER

Lord, I know that the choice is
mine—I can either count
my blessings or recount my
disappointments. Today, help me
to focus my thoughts upon
my blessings, my gifts,
and my opportunities.
Amen

CHAPTER 14

Honesty Is the Best Policy

Tell each other the truth because we all belong to each other . . . .

Ephesians 4:25 ICB

TODAY'S BIG IDEA!

No matter where you happen to be, be honest. And play fair.

Whether you're playing sports or working in the classroom, or anywhere else for that matter, it's important to be honest. When you tell the truth, you'll feel better about yourself, and other people will feel better about you, too. But that's not all. When you tell the truth, God knows—and He will reward you for your honesty.

Telling the truth is hard sometimes. But it's better to be honest, even when it's hard. So remember this: telling the truth is always the right thing to do . . . always.

**The single most important
element in any human relationship
is honesty—with oneself,
with God, and with others.**

—

Catherine Marshall

You cannot glorify Christ
and practice dishonesty
at the same time.

—

Warren Wiersbe

God doesn't expect you
to be perfect, but he does insist on
complete honesty.

—

Rick Warren

NOW HEAR THIS!

All my life I tried to be honest with people. I wish I had been a little more honest with myself.

—

Mickey Mantle

DID YOU KNOW?

Wrigley Field, home of the Chicago Cubs, was opened in 1916. It was originally called Weeghman Park (named for the man who, at the time, was the team's major owner). The Cubs were later acquired by chewing gum magnate William Wrigley, who renamed the ballpark for himself.

ONE MORE THING TO REMEMBER

Honesty is the best policy. Make sure that it's your policy, even when telling the truth makes you feel a little uncomfortable.

TODAY'S PRAYER

Dear Lord, I know that it's important to be an honest person. Since I want other people to be truthful with me, let me be truthful with them, today and every day.
Amen

CHAPTER 15

Be a Team Player

*You're blessed when you can show
people how to cooperate instead
of compete or fight.*
Matthew 5:9 MSG

TODAY'S BIG IDEA!

Teamwork works. Selfishness doesn't.

As you play the game of baseball (or the game of life), you need teammates. And when you think about it, being a good teammate is simple: It just means that you're willing to help the other kids on your team become better players.

Helping other people can be fun! When you help others, you feel better about yourself—and you know that God approves of what you're doing. And when you cooperate with your family, with your friends, and with your teammates, you'll soon discover that it's more fun when everybody works together. So do everybody (including yourself) a big favor: Learn better ways to share and better ways to cooperate. When you do, everybody wins.

How many people stop
because so few say, "Go!"

—

Charles Swindoll

A lot of people have gone further
than they thought they could
because someone else
thought they could.

—

Zig Ziglar

Enthusiasm, like the flu,
is contagious—
we get it from one another.

—

Barbara Johnson

Encouraging others means
helping people, looking for
the best in them, and trying to
bring out their positive qualities.

—

John Maxwell

NOW HEAR THIS!

You can always take what you have and make it better.

—

Ted Williams

My formula for success was simple: practice, practice, practice.

—

Ted Williams

DID YOU KNOW?

One record that many folks thought might never be broken was George Sisler's long-standing mark of 257 hits in a single season. But Ichiro Suzuki broke that record in 2004 with 259 hits. Sisler's mark had been on the books for 84 long years. Do you think Ichiro's will last that long?

ONE MORE THING TO REMEMBER

You can do things to make your teammates better players, and they can do things to make you a better player, too. So don't be a selfish ballplayer. Think of the team first, not yourself.

TODAY'S PRAYER

Dear Lord, help me be a team player today and every day. Let me look for the best in my teammates, and help me be more interested in my team's success than I am in my own success.
Amen

CHAPTER 16

On the Diamond or Off, Be Thankful

*Be cheerful no matter what;
pray all the time; thank God no matter
what happens. This is the way God wants
you who belong to Christ Jesus to live.*
1 Thessalonians 5:16-18 MSG

TODAY'S BIG IDEA!

It's important to be thankful for all your opportunities, including the opportunity to enjoy sports like baseball.

He was a teammate of Babe Ruth and perhaps the greatest first baseman of all time. His name was Lou Gehrig, and while he was still playing ball, he contracted a terrible disease with the initials ALS (today, lots of people refer to this condition as "Lou Gehrig's Disease"). Despite being very sick, Gehrig made a famous speech at Yankee Stadium, during which he said, "I consider myself the luckiest man on the face of the earth." All of us should be that thankful.

Are you like Lou Gehrig? Do you count your blessings, not your troubles? If so, congratulations!

Today, while you're standing at the plate, give thanks for that opportunity and then take your swings. Because if you are playing the game of baseball or the game of life—and if you're thankful for the opportunity to play that game—you win.

Thanksgiving or complaining—
these words express two contrastive
attitudes of the souls of God's
children in regard to His dealings
with them. The soul that gives
thanks can find comfort in
everything; the soul that complains
can find comfort in nothing.

—

Hannah Whitall Smith

Thanksgiving is good
but Thanksliving is better.

—

Jim Gallery

The words "thank" and "think"
come from the same root word.
If we would think more,
we would thank more.

—

Warren Wiersbe

It is always possible to be thankful
for what is given rather than
to complain about what is not given.
One or the other becomes
a habit of life.

—

Elisabeth Elliot

NOW HEAR THIS!

I consider myself the luckiest man
on the face of the earth. I may have been
given a bad break, but with all this,
I have a lot to live for.

—

Lou Gehrig

Enthusiasm has to be generated
day in and day out. It's the only way
to play winning baseball.

—

Earl Weaver

DID YOU KNOW?

During his amazing career, hard-throwing Nolan Ryan recorded an astounding seven no-hitters. That's a pitching record that may never be broken.

ONE MORE THING TO REMEMBER

Every day, God gives us cause to rejoice. The rest is up to us.

TODAY'S PRAYER

Dear Lord, I am a very lucky person,
and I thank You for my blessings.
Help me to be a good person,
and help me use my talents for
Your glory . . . and for Your Son.
Amen

CHAPTER 17

Respect the Rules . . . And Play Fair!

It's quite simple: Do what is fair and just to your neighbor, be compassionate and loyal in your love, and don't take yourself too seriously—take God seriously.

Micah 6:8 MSG

TODAY'S BIG IDEA!

God has rules (which you should always try to obey) and the game of baseball has rules, too. You're never too young to play by the rules.

When you're playing sports, do you try to obey the rules? And do you try to obey God's rules all day long, every day? Hopefully so!

An attitude of obedience starts in your heart and works its way out from there. That's why it's important to listen to your heart when it tells you how to behave. When you do, you'll be happier, healthier, smarter, and safer.

So don't forget to listen to your parents and your coaches. And don't forget to listen to your conscience. When you listen carefully, you'll obey the rules . . . and you'll make everybody glad, including yourself!

There may be no trumpet sound or loud applause when we make a right decision, just a calm sense of resolution and peace.

—

Gloria Gaither

He leads us in the paths of righteousness wherever we are placed.

—

Oswald Chambers

Don't worry about what you
do not understand. Worry about
what you do understand
in the Bible but do not live by.

—

Corrie ten Boom

Although God causes all things
to work together for good for
His children, He still holds us
accountable for our behavior.

—

Kay Arthur

NOW HEAR THIS!

If you work hard every day and work hard on every play, people notice, and word gets around.

—

Tommy John

Always run them out. You can never tell.

—

Joe McCarthy

DID YOU KNOW?

The last player to bat .400 for a full season in the major leagues was Ted Williams. Williams, who was one of the greatest players who ever lived, achieved that feat in 1941.

ONE MORE THING TO REMEMBER

Remember: Rules aren't made to be broken. Rules are made to be obeyed!

TODAY'S PRAYER

Dear Lord, when I play by Your rules, You bless my life. But, when I disobey Your rules, I suffer the consequences. Help me play by the rules today and every day. Amen

CHAPTER 18

Blaming Others . . .

An angry person causes trouble.
Proverbs 29:22 NCV

TODAY'S BIG IDEA!

If you run into problems on the ball field, you may be tempted to blame your teammates (or the umpire). But don't start spreading the blame—the blame game only leads to trouble.

When something goes wrong, do you look for somebody to blame? And do you try to blame other people even if you're the one who made the mistake? Hopefully not!

In the game of baseball (and in the game of life) it's tempting to blame everybody (except yourself!). But the blame game is a game with no winners. So if things aren't going your way, don't look for somebody to blame; look for some way to make things better. Because playing the blame game doesn't work, and while you're playing it, neither do you.

**You'll never win the blame game,
so why even bother to play?**

—

Marie T. Freeman

**There comes a time when we simply
have to face the challenges in our
lives and stop backing down.**

—

John Eldredge

**The main thing is this:
we should never blame anyone
or anything for our defeats.**

—

A. W. Tozer

NOW HEAR THIS!

Make optimism a way of life.

—

Brooks Robinson

**I became an optimist when
I discovered that I wasn't going
to win any more games
by being anything else.**

—

Earl Weaver

DID YOU KNOW?

Ty Cobb's lifetime batting average is a baseball record that will probably never be broken. In a career that lasted from 1905 to 1928, Cobb hit for a .366 average. Today's best players are fortunate if they can hit for that high an average once in a career. Ty averaged it over a 23-year career.

ONE MORE THING TO REMEMBER

Don't try to blame other people for the mistakes you make. When you point your finger at someone else, the rest of your fingers are pointing back at you!

TODAY'S PRAYER

Dear Lord, when I make a mistake,
I want to admit it. Help me not blame
others for the mistakes that I make.
And when I make a mistake,
help me to learn from it.
Amen

CHAPTER 19

Play by the Golden Rule

*Therefore, whatever you want others
to do for you, do also the same for them—
this is the Law and the Prophets.*

Matthew 7:12 Holman CSB

TODAY'S BIG IDEA!

Practice makes perfect. So make sure you always practice the Golden Rule!

When you're playing baseball, it's important to know the rules. And when you're trying to live a good life, it's essential to know God's rules. Jesus told us that we should treat other people in the same way that we would want to be treated: that's the Golden Rule—and it's a rule that you should obey every day.

God wants you to treat other people with respect, kindness, courtesy, and love. When you do, you make your family, your friends, and your teammates happy . . . and you make your Father in heaven very proud.

So if you're wondering how to treat someone else, ask the person you see every time you look into the mirror. The answer you receive will tell you exactly what to do.

The Golden Rule starts at home, but it should never stop there.

—

Marie T. Freeman

When you add value to others, you do not take anything away from yourself.

—

John Maxwell

No one stands taller in the climb
to success than when he bends over
to help up someone else.

—

John Maxwell

Doing something positive toward
another person is a practical
approach to feeling good
about yourself.

—

Barbara Johnson

NOW HEAR THIS!

Every day is a new opportunity.
That's the way life is, with a new game
every day, and that's the way baseball is.

—

Bob Feller

I would be lost without baseball.
I don't think I could stand being away
from it as long as I was alive.

—

Roberto Clemente

DID YOU KNOW?

Johnny Burnett still holds the record for the most hits in a single major league game. In 1932, while playing in an 18-inning game for Cleveland, Burnett made nine hits (he went 9 for 11). Who's going to top that?

ONE MORE THING TO REMEMBER

What's good for you is good for them, too. If you want others to treat you according to the Golden Rule, then you should be quick to treat them in the same way. In other words, always play by the rule: the Golden Rule.

TODAY'S PRAYER

Dear Lord, help me to always
do my very best to treat others
as I wish to be treated.
The Golden Rule is Your rule, Father;
let me also make it mine.
Amen

CHAPTER 20

Be Ready to Serve!

Sitting down, He called the Twelve and said to them, "If anyone wants to be first, he must be last of all and servant of all."

Mark 9:35 Holman CSB

TODAY'S BIG IDEA!

Wherever you happen to be—whatever your age, whatever your circumstances—you can find people to serve and ways to serve. So what are you waiting for?

He was a star in football, baseball, basketball, and track. And on April 15, 1947, when he took the field for the Brooklyn Dodgers, he broke major league baseball's color barrier. He was Jackie Robinson, a man who became a role model for millions of Americans, both black and white.

Robinson said, "A life is not important except for the impact it has on other lives." And he was right. So if you'd like to make a major-league impact on your world, be quick to offer a helping hand or an encouraging word. When you do, you can be sure you, like Jackie Robinson, will be a major-league winner.

No life can surpass that of
a person who quietly continues
to serve God in the place
where fate has placed him.

—

C. H. Spurgeon

We are only fully alive when
we're helping others.

—

Rick Warren

**If you aren't serving,
you're just existing, because
life is meant for ministry.**

—

Rick Warren

**Have thy tools ready;
God will find thee work.**

—

Charles Kingsley

NOW HEAR THIS!

Problems are the price
you pay for progress.

—

Branch Rickey

DID YOU KNOW?

In the earliest days of baseball, the ball was less lively and the ballparks usually had very large outfields. So home runs were hard to come by, and most homers were inside-the-park round trippers. Today, inside-the-park homers are rare, but over-the-fence homeruns are most certainly not. Times change, and so does baseball.

ONE MORE THING TO REMEMBER

You can make a difference: If you choose to serve, you'll be doing the world (and yourself) a big favor.

TODAY'S PRAYER

Dear Lord, let me help others in every way that I can. Jesus served others; I can too. I will serve other people with my good deeds and with my prayers, and I will give thanks for all those who serve and protect our nation and our world.

Amen

CHAPTER 21

Be Patient

Always be humble and gentle.
Be patient and accept each other
with love.

Ephesians 4:2 ICB

TODAY'S BIG IDEA!

The best hitters are usually patient at the plate; they wait for a good pitch to hit. So be patient! After all, the Bible says that patience pays, and the Bible is always right.

The dictionary defines the word "patience" as "the ability to be calm, tolerant, and understanding." Here's what that means: the word "calm" means being in control of your emotions (not letting your emotions control you). The word "tolerant" means being kind and considerate to people who are different from you. And, the word "understanding" means being able to put yourself in another person's shoes.

If you can be calm, tolerant, and understanding—both on the baseball field and off—you will be the kind of person whose good deeds are a blessing to your family, to your friends, to your coaches, and to your teammates. And that's exactly the kind of person that God wants you to be.

The next time you're disappointed,
don't panic. Don't give up.
Just be patient and let God remind
you he's still in control.

—

Max Lucado

Patience is the companion
of wisdom.

—

St. Augustine

God gave everyone patience—
wise people use it.

—

Anonymous

Our Lord worked with people
as they were, and He was patient—
not tolerant of sin,
but compassionate.

—

Vance Havner

NOW HEAR THIS!

**You just can't beat the person
who never gives up.**

—

Babe Ruth

**They say it can't be done,
but that doesn't always work out.**

—

Casey Stengel

DID YOU KNOW?

The oldest man ever to play in a professional baseball game was the legendary pitcher Satchel Paige. In 1965, at the age of 59, he pitched in one game for the Kansas City Athletics. Satchel tossed three innings, allowed no runs, and struck out one batter.

ONE MORE THING TO REMEMBER

If you think you're about to say or do something you'll regret later, slow down and take a deep breath, or two deep breaths, or ten, or . . . well you get the idea.

TODAY'S PRAYER

Dear Lord, sometimes it's hard to be
patient, and that's exactly when
I should try my hardest to be patient.
Help me to obey You by being
a patient, loving person . . .
even when it's hard.
Amen

CHAPTER 22

Don't Be a Chronic Excuse-maker

If you hide your sins, you will not succeed.
Proverbs 28:13 NCV

TODAY'S BIG IDEA!

When things don't go well for you, it's tempting to make excuses. But excuses don't win games and they don't win fans, either. So forget the excuses and think about the next play, not the last one.

What is an excuse? Well, when you make up an excuse, that means that you try to come up with a good reason that you didn't do something that you should have done.

Anybody can make up excuses, and you can too. But you shouldn't get into the habit of making too many excuses. Why? Because excuses don't work in baseball or in life. And why don't they work? Because everybody has already heard so many excuses that almost everybody can recognize excuses when they hear them.

So the next time you're tempted to make up an excuse, don't. Instead of making an excuse, do what you think is right. After all, the very best excuse of all . . . is no excuse.

Replace your excuses
with fresh determination.

—

Charles Swindoll

We need to stop focusing
on our lacks and stop giving out
excuses and start looking at
and listening to Jesus.

—

Anne Graham Lotz

An excuse is only the skin
of a reason stuffed with a lie.

—

Vance Havner

Making up a string of excuses is
usually harder than doing the work.

—

Marie T. Freeman

NOW HEAR THIS!

Keep your excuses to yourself.

—

Christy Mathewson

There is always some kid who may be seeing me for the first time or last time. I owe him my best.

—

Joe DiMaggio

DID YOU KNOW?

Legendary Yankee first baseman Lou Gehrig played in 2,130 consecutive games. That record stood until Cal Ripken of the Orioles broke it in 1995. Ripken raised the bar to 2,632 consecutive games. Wow.

ONE MORE THING TO REMEMBER

The habit of making excuses is a bad habit. Excuses lead to trouble. If you're in the habit of making excuses, the best day to stop that habit is today.

TODAY'S PRAYER

Dear Lord, when I'm tempted to make excuses, help me to be strong as I accept responsibility for my actions.
Amen

CHAPTER 23

Be a Good Loser and a Good Winner

Keep your eyes focused on what is right, and look straight ahead to what is good. Be careful what you do, and always do what is right. Don't turn off the road of goodness; keep away from evil paths.

Proverbs 4:25-27 NCV

TODAY'S BIG IDEA!

Some kids may try to convince you that winning is the most important thing. But the Bible makes it clear that doing what's right is far more important than winning a game.

Okay, since you're a baseball player, it's safe to say that you'd rather play on a winning team. After all, who really likes to lose? Nobody! But here's a question for you to think about: How important is winning? The answer is: It depends.

If you're winning friends for Jesus, or if you're winning against the temptation to do something wrong, then winning is very important. But when comes to everyday sporting events (like baseball games), winning isn't as important as you might think.

So the next time your team ends up on the losing end of the score, keep things in perspective . . . and don't be too upset. After all, sporting events come and go, and there's always another baseball game to play if you're willing to lace up your cleats. But the really important things in life—like your relationship with God and His Son—last forever. And the eternal victories are the ones that really matter.

Don't let the world define success
for you. Only God can do that.

—

Jim Gallery

Victory is the result of Christ's life
lived out in the believer.
It is important to see that this
kind of victory, not defeat,
is God's purpose for His children.

—

Corrie ten Boom

We can be victorious,
but only if we walk with God.

—

Beth Moore

Never forget:
If you belong to the King,
you are on the winning side.

—

Billy Graham

NOW HEAR THIS!

You can learn little from victory.
You can learn everything from defeat.

—

Christy Mathewson

There are bad days and good days,
bad months and good months,
bad years and good years.
If you lose, pick yourself up and carry on.
That's baseball, and that's life.

—

Tim McCarver

DID YOU KNOW?

Only two major league players have hit into four double plays in a single game. One of those players, Joe Torre, turned out to be a great player and great manager, too.

ONE MORE THING TO REMEMBER

If you want to be a winner, just try your hardest and be a good sport. When you do, you'll always be a winner, even if your team doesn't score the most runs.

TODAY'S PRAYER

Dear Lord, help me remember that there are many things in life that are more important than winning baseball games. Help me understand what's really important, Lord, this day and every day.
Amen

CHAPTER 24

You Can Do It . . . If You Stick to It!

Finishing is better than starting.
Patience is better than pride.

Ecclesiastes 7:8 NLT

TODAY'S BIG IDEA!

If you want to be a champion, you can't give up at the first sign of trouble. So if at first you don't succeed, keep trying until you do.

In baseball and in life, the way you think determines the way you play. If you think you can do something, then you can probably do it. If you think you can't do something, then you probably won't do it.

So remember this: if you're having a little trouble getting something done, don't get mad, don't get frustrated, don't get discouraged, and don't give up. Just keep trying . . . and believe in yourself.

When you try hard—and keep trying hard—you can really do amazing things . . . but if you quit at the first sign of trouble, you'll miss out. So here's a good rule to follow: when you have something that you want to finish, finish it . . . and finish it sooner rather than later.

Keep advancing; do not stop, do not turn back, do not turn from the straight road.

—

St. Augustine

Perseverance is more than endurance. It is endurance combined with absolute assurance and certainty that what we are looking for is going to happen.

—

Oswald Chambers

Some people gear up for
a sprint when they need to train
for the marathon.

—

Bill Hybels

By perseverance
the snail reached the ark.

—

C. H. Spurgeon

NOW HEAR THIS!

Never let your head hang down.
Never give up and sit down and grieve.
Find another way.

—

Satchel Paige

My motto was always to keep swinging.
Whether I was in a slump, or feeling badly,
or having trouble off the field,
the only thing to do was keep swinging.

—

Hank Aaron

DID YOU KNOW?

The player who lasted longest in major-league baseball was Nolan Ryan. He played for an amazing 27 seasons!

ONE MORE THING TO REMEMBER

If things don't work out at first, don't quit. If you don't keep trying, you'll never know how good you can be.

TODAY'S PRAYER

Dear Lord, sometimes I feel like giving up. When I feel that way, help me do the right thing . . . and help me finish the work You want me to do.
Amen

CHAPTER 25

Watch What You Say!

Pleasant words are like a honeycomb.
They make a person happy and healthy.
Proverbs 16:24 ICB

TODAY'S BIG IDEA!

When you're at the ballpark (or anyplace else, for that matter), you should pay careful attention to the things you say and the way you say them. After all, your friends are listening . . . and so is God!

Are you careful about the things you say, on the field or off? If your answer is yes, that's good because the words you speak are important. If you speak kind words, you make other people feel better. And that's exactly what God wants you to do!

How hard is it to say a kind word? Not very! Yet sometimes we're so busy that we forget to say the very things that might make other people feel better.

Kind words help; cruel words hurt. It's as simple as that. And, when we say the right thing at the right time, we give a gift that can change somebody's game, somebody's day, or somebody's life.

Attitude and the spirit in which
we communicate are as important
as the words we say.

—

Charles Stanley

Change the heart,
and you change the speech.

—

Warren Wiersbe

The great test of a person's
character is his tongue.

—

Oswald Chambers

If you can't think of something
nice to say, keep thinking.

—

Criswell Freeman

NOW HEAR THIS!

**Dad always said,
"Practice, practice, practice."
Dad was right. Practice paid off.**

—

Mickey Mantle

DID YOU KNOW?

The most famous perfect game in baseball history was pitched by Don Larsen of the New York Yankees in the 1956 World Series. Larsen threw only 97 pitches, and not a single opponent from the Brooklyn Dodgers reached first base.

ONE MORE THING TO REMEMBER

If you can't think of something nice to say, keep thinking (and keep quiet) until you can think of the right words. It's better to say nothing than to hurt someone's feelings.

TODAY'S PRAYER

Dear Lord, You hear every word that I say. Help me remember to speak words that are honest, kind, and helpful.
Amen

CHAPTER 26

You Don't Have to Be Perfect!

Jesus said,
"Don't let your hearts be troubled.
Trust in God, and trust in me."
John 14:1 NCV

TODAY'S BIG IDEA!

In sports and in life, it's always good to improve your skills. But you don't have to be perfect. So if you make a mistake (or two), don't be upset. When you've tried your hardest and done your best, be satisfied.

If you're trying to be a perfect baseball player or a perfect person, you're trying to do something that's impossible. No matter how much you try, you can't be perfect . . . and that's okay.

God doesn't expect you to live a mistake-free life—and neither should you. In the game of life, God expects you to try, but He doesn't always expect you to win. Sometimes, you'll make mistakes, but even then, you shouldn't give up!

So remember this: you don't have to be perfect to be a good person. In fact, you don't even need to be "almost-perfect." You simply must try your best and leave the rest up to God.

**What makes a Christian
a Christian is not perfection
but forgiveness.**

—

Max Lucado

The happiest people in the world
are not those who have no problems,
but the people who have learned
to live with things that are
less than perfect.

—

James Dobson

God doesn't expect you to live
a mistake-free life—
and neither should you.

—

Criswell Freeman

NOW HEAR THIS!

If the world was perfect, it wouldn't be.

—

Yogi Berra

DID YOU KNOW?

In 1959, Harvey Haddux, a pitcher for the Pittsburgh Pirates, pitched 12 innings perfectly (not a single player from the opposing Milwaukee Braves reached first base). But Haddux's team couldn't score a run, so the score remained 0-0. Finally in the 13th inning, the Braves scored and Haddux became the losing pitcher. This just proves that even if you play a near-perfect game, you may not always win.

ONE MORE THING TO REMEMBER

If you hear a little voice inside your head telling you that you'll never be good enough . . . don't pay attention to that little voice. God loves you . . . and if you're good enough for God, you're good enough.

TODAY'S PRAYER

Dear Lord, help me remember that I don't have to be perfect to be wonderful.
Amen

CHAPTER 27

Listen to Your Coach

The wise are glad to be instructed.

Proverbs 10:8 NLT

TODAY'S BIG IDEA!

Your coach deserves to be treated respectfully, and so do the umpires. And it's up to you to give them the respect they deserve.

Are you polite and respectful to your parents, your teachers, and your coaches? And do you do your best to treat everybody with the respect they deserve? If you want to obey God's rules, then you should be able to answer yes to these questions.

Remember this: the Bible teaches you to be a respectful person—and if it's right there in the Bible, it's certainly the right thing to do!

Great leaders understand that
the right attitude will set
the right atmosphere, which enables
the right response from others.

—

John Maxwell

The next best thing to being wise
oneself is to live in a circle
of those who are.

—

C. S. Lewis

When God wants to accomplish
something, He calls dedicated men
and women to challenge
His people and lead the way.

—

Warren Wiersbe

The alternative to discipline
is disaster.

—

Vance Havner

NOW HEAR THIS!

Don't be afraid to take advice.
There's always something
new to learn.

—

Babe Ruth

DID YOU KNOW?

Today, professional baseball players move around a lot. But in the old days, the best players usually stayed put. The record for the most consecutive seasons played with the same team is 23, shared by Brooks Robinson (Baltimore Orioles) and Carl Yastrzemski (Boston Red Sox). That's almost a quarter of a century playing baseball in the same city . . . sounds like fun!

ONE MORE THING TO REMEMBER

When it comes to baseball, you can be sure that your coach knows more than you do . . . so listen and learn.

TODAY'S PRAYER

Dear Lord, give me the maturity to respect my teachers, my coaches, and my parents, today and every day.
Amen

CHAPTER 28

Don't Get Mad . . . Play Harder

My dear brothers, always be willing to listen and slow to speak. Do not become angry easily. Anger will not help you live a good life as God wants.

James 1:19 ICB

TODAY'S BIG IDEA!

When things don't go your way, you may be tempted to become angry. Very angry. But if you're wise, you'll learn to control your anger before it controls you.

Sometimes, when you're playing baseball, you may get angry. Either you make a mistake or somebody else does, and you feel your temper starting to boil. When you become angry, you may say something or do something that you'll regret later. That's why you should learn to control your anger before it controls you.

Jesus does not intend that you strike out against other people, and He doesn't intend that your heart be troubled by anger. Your heart should instead be filled with love, just like Jesus' heart was . . . and is!

**When you strike out in anger,
you may miss the other person,
but you will always hit yourself.**

—

Jim Gallery

When something robs you of your
peace of mind, ask yourself if it is
worth the energy you are expending
on it. If not, then put it out of
your mind in an act of discipline.
Every time the thought of
"it" returns, refuse it.

—

Kay Arthur

Is there somebody who's always
getting your goat?
Talk to the Shepherd.

—

Anonymous

NOW HEAR THIS!

**Everything is possible to him
who dares.**

—

A. G. Spalding

**Take care of your body.
You've only got one.**

—

Mickey Mantle

DID YOU KNOW?

In 1973, Ron Blomberg became the first designated hitter in major league baseball. Soon thereafter, Tony Oliva became the first DH to hit a home run.

ONE MORE THING TO REMEMBER

Time Out: If you become angry, the time to step away from the situation is before you say unkind words or do unkind things—not after. It's perfectly okay to place yourself in "time out" until you can calm down.

TODAY'S PRAYER

Lord, when I become angry, help me to remember that You offer me peace. Let me turn to You for wisdom, for patience, and for the peace that only You can give. Amen

CHAPTER 29

You've Got Lots to Learn

Remember what you are taught.
And listen carefully to words of knowledge.

Proverbs 23:12 ICB

TODAY'S BIG IDEA!

Your coach has lots to teach you, but you can't learn much while you're talking. So when your coach is talking, make sure that you're listening.

Do you know all there is to know about baseball . . . or about anything else, for that matter? Of course you don't! Even if you've already learned a lot, there's still more to learn—on the field and off.

When it comes to learning life's lessons, you can either do things the easy way or the hard way. The easy way can be summed up as follows: when you're supposed to learn something, you learn it the first time! Unfortunately, lots of people (but hopefully not you) learn much more slowly than that.

So today and every day, do yourself a big favor by learning your lessons sooner rather than later. Because the sooner you do, the sooner you can move on to the next lesson and the next and the next.

Knowledge is power.

—

Francis Bacon

The more wisdom enters our hearts,
the more we will be able to trust
our hearts in difficult situations.

—

John Eldredge

The doorstep to the temple
of wisdom is a knowledge
of our own ignorance.

—

C. H. Spurgeon

It's the things you learn after
you know it all that really count.

—

Vance Havner

NOW HEAR THIS!

**In baseball, I learn something
new every day. Every day
and every game is different.**

—

Don Baylor

**When you're through learning,
you're through.**

—

Vernon Law

DID YOU KNOW?

In 1941, Joe DiMagio of the Yankees got a hit in 56 straight games. That record still stands, and in today's high-pressure world, it will be very hard to break.

ONE MORE THING TO REMEMBER

When you listen to the things your coach has to say, it shows that you care. Listening carefully is not just the courteous thing to do; it's also the respectful thing to do.

TODAY'S PRAYER

Dear Lord, make me a good listener, especially when I'm listening to people who have much to teach me. Amen

CHAPTER 30

Wherever You Go, Follow Jesus

And whatever you do, in word or in deed, do everything in the name of the Lord Jesus, giving thanks to God the Father through Him.

Colossians 3:17 Holman CSB

TODAY'S BIG IDEA!

Don't take sports too seriously! Whether your team wins or loses isn't really that important. What is important, of course, is that you walk with Jesus every day of your life.

The most important thing you'll ever do in your life has nothing to do with baseball. The most important thing you'll ever do in your life is to make the decision to follow Jesus wherever He leads you.

Jesus wants to have a real relationship with you. Are you willing to have a meaningful relationship with Him? Unless you can answer this question with a great big "Yes," you may miss out on some wonderful things.

This day offers yet another opportunity to behave yourself like a real Christian. When you do, God will guide your steps and bless your life . . . forever.

We have in Jesus Christ a perfect
example of how to put
God's truth into practice.

—

Bill Bright

A disciple is a follower of Christ.
That means you take on
His priorities as your own.
His agenda becomes your agenda.
His mission becomes your mission.

—

Charles Stanley

It is God to whom and with whom
we travel; while He is the End
of our journey, He is also
at every stopping place.

—

Elisabeth Elliot

The essence of the Christian life is
Jesus: that in all things He might
have the preeminence,
not that in some things
He might have a place.

—

Franklin Graham

NOW HEAR THIS!

I'd like to finish it by saying
to all you kids: Take good care
of yourself and go out there
and make us proud.

—

Mickey Mantle

DID YOU KNOW?

The longest standing single season record
in major league baseball is for the highest
batting average. It's an amazingly high average
of .426, posted by Nap Lajoie way back
in 1901. And who knows, that record may
last for another hundred years!

ONE MORE THING TO REMEMBER

If you want to be a little more like Christ . . .
learn about His teachings, follow in His foot-
steps, and obey His commandments.

TODAY'S PRAYER

Dear Lord, You sent Jesus to save
the world and to save me.
I thank You for Jesus,
and I will do my best to follow Him,
today and forever.
Amen

Bible Verses to
Remember

**Cast your burden
on the Lord, and He will
support you;
He will never allow
the righteous to be shaken.**

—

Psalm 55:22 Holman CSB

A friend loves at all times, and a brother is born for a difficult time.

—

Proverbs 17:17 Holman CSB

*For God so loved
the world, that he gave
his only begotten Son,
that whosoever believeth
in him should not perish,
but have everlasting life.*
—

John 3:16 KJV

Do not worry about anything. But pray and ask God for everything you need.

Philippians 4:6 ICB

*I give you a new
commandment:
that you love one another.
Just as I have loved you,
you should also
love one another.*

—

John 13:34 Holman CSB

If someone does wrong to you, do not pay him back by doing wrong to him.

—

Romans 12:17 ICB

Now these three remain:
faith, hope, and love.
But the greatest of these
is love.

—

1 Corinthians 13:13 Holman CSB

Finishing is better than starting. Patience is better than pride.

—

Ecclesiastes 7:8 NLT

My Team Photo

My Team

As a way to remember your baseball teammates, jot down some notes on the following pages.

Team Name:

Year:

Coach's Name:

Phone Number:

E-mail Address:

Something Cool to Remember:

Name:

Position:

Phone Number:

E-mail Address:

Something Cool to Remember:

Name:

Position:

Phone Number:

E-mail Address:

Something Cool to Remember:

Name:

Position:

Phone Number:

E-mail Address:

Something Cool to Remember:

Name:

Position:

Phone Number:

E-mail Address:

Something Cool to Remember:

Name:

Position:

Phone Number:

E-mail Address:

Something Cool to Remember:

Name:

Position:

Phone Number:

E-mail Address:

Something Cool to Remember:

Name:

Position:

Phone Number:

E-mail Address:

Something Cool to Remember:

Name:

Position:

Phone Number:

E-mail Address:

Something Cool to Remember:

Name:

Position:

Phone Number:

E-mail Address:

Something Cool to Remember:

Name:

Position:

Phone Number:

E-mail Address:

Something Cool to Remember:

Name:

Position:

Phone Number:

E-mail Address:

Something Cool to Remember:

Name:

Position:

Phone Number:

E-mail Address:

Something Cool to Remember:

Name:

Position:

Phone Number:

E-mail Address:

Something Cool to Remember:

Name:

Position:

Phone Number:

E-mail Address:

Something Cool to Remember:

Name:

Position:

Phone Number:

E-mail Address:

Something Cool to Remember:

Name:

Position:

Phone Number:

E-mail Address:

Something Cool to Remember:

For when the one Great Scorer
comes to write against
your name, He marks not
that you won or lost,
but how you played the game.

—

Grantland Rice